EMERGENCY 999!
AMBULANCE

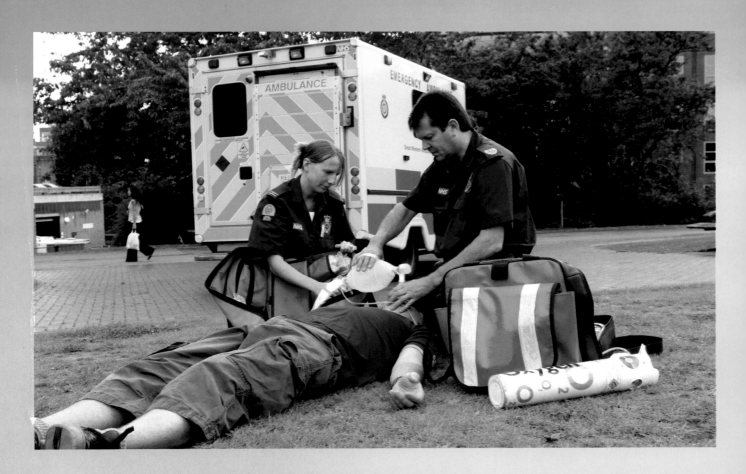

Kathryn Walker

Photography by Chris Fairclough

Published in 2013 by Wayland

Copyright © Wayland 2013

Wayland
338 Euston Road
London NW1 3BH

Wayland Australia
Level 17/207 Kent Street
Sydney, NSW 2000

Produced for Wayland by Discovery Books Ltd
Wayland series editor: Katie Powell
Editor: James Nixon
Designer: Ian Winton
Commissioned photography: Chris Fairclough

The author, publisher and Discovery Books Ltd would like to thank Great Western
Ambulance Service for their help and participation in this book.

Picture credits: Fastaid: p. 22 bottom; Great Western Ambulance Service: pp. 5 top, 6
bottom, 7, 8, 9, 10 top, 12, 13 bottom, 14, 15, 17 top, 18 bottom, 19 bottom, 20, 21 top, 22 top,
26, 28; London Ambulance Service: pp. 11, 13 top, 23, 24, 25; Shutterstock: pp. 5 bottom
(Laurens Parsons Photography), 6 top (iofoto), 21 bottom (Keith Publicover), 29 (Shane White).

British Library Cataloguing in Publication Data
Walker, Kathryn, 1957-
   Ambulance service. -- (Emergency 999)
   1. Ambulance service--Juvenile literature. 2. Assistance
   in emergencies--Juvenile literature.
   I. Title II. Series
   362.1'88-dc22
   ISBN: 978 0 7502 8204 8

Printed in China

10 9 8 7 6 5 4 3 2 1

Wayland is a division of Hachette Children's Books,
an Hachette UK company, www.hachette.co.uk

Note to parents and teachers: Every effort has been made by the Publishers to ensure that
the websites in this book are suitable for children, that they are of the highest educational
value, and that they contain no inappropriate or offensive material. However, because of the
nature of the Internet, it is impossible to guarantee that the contents of these sites will not be
altered. We strongly advise that Internet access is supervised by a responsible adult.

CONTENTS

MEDICAL EMERGENCY!

When someone is ill or hurt, they usually go to the doctor or to the **Accident and Emergency (A&E)** unit of a hospital. But if a person suddenly becomes very ill or is badly injured in an accident, it is an emergency and they need help fast!

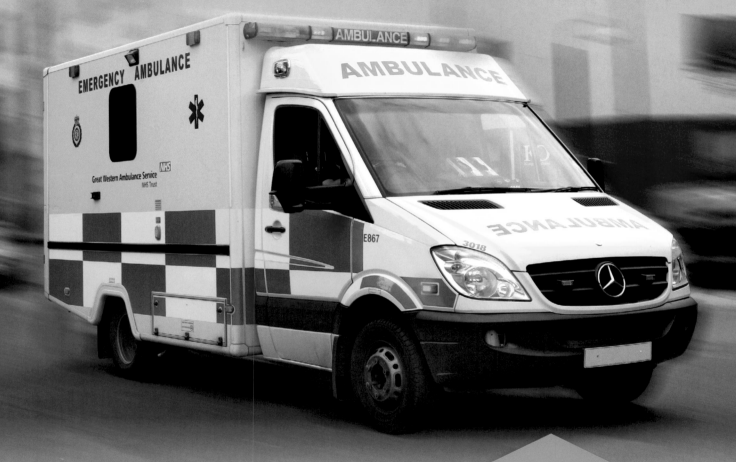

In a medical emergency you need to phone 999 or 112 and ask for the ambulance service. They will send out a **paramedic.** Paramedics are trained to give medical treatment and will take the patient to hospital if necessary.

An ambulance carries life-saving equipment and is designed to take patients quickly and safely to hospital.

When to call

We need to call the ambulance service if illness or injury is putting someone's life in danger. If you think the casualty might become worse, and there isn't time to get them to hospital, call for an ambulance.

If you think that the patient has broken bones, moving the person yourself could make the injury much worse. Again, it is time to ring 999 for expert help.

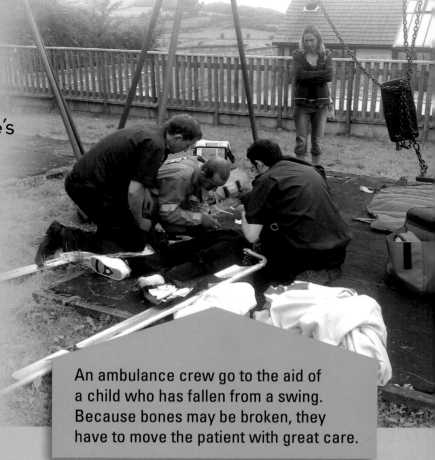

An ambulance crew go to the aid of a child who has fallen from a swing. Because bones may be broken, they have to move the patient with great care.

Dorset Fire & Rescue
In Partnership with
Dorset Ambulance
NHS Trust

Oxygen

999 Notes

You should call the ambulance service if someone:
- has severe chest pain
- suddenly has problems talking or breathing
- is losing a lot of blood
- is **unconscious** – or losing consciousness.

A paramedic checks the **pulse** of an unconscious patient.

CALLING FOR HELP

When you phone 999, an operator answers and asks which emergency service you need. In a medical emergency, you say 'ambulance'.

The operator then puts your call through to the ambulance dispatch centre. A call handler there will first ask you where the emergency is. Then he or she will want your telephone number and will ask what the problem is. As soon as the call handler knows where and what the emergency is, the nearest ambulance is alerted.

When dialling 999, it is important to stay calm so that the call handler can get a clear picture of the situation.

Important questions

The call handler then asks more questions. Answering these is important and will not delay paramedic help getting to you. It will give the ambulance crew more information about the emergency. The call handler may also give you **first aid** advice while help is on the way.

The call handler will ask:
- Are you with the patient?
- How many people are hurt or sick?
- How old is the patient? (You may have to make a guess.)
- Is the patient male or female?
- Is the patient **conscious**?
- Is the patient breathing?

At the ambulance dispatch centre, the call handler logs details of the emergency on the computer system.

999 Notes

When you call from a **landline**, a map showing where you are calling from comes up on the call handler's computer screen. The same thing does not happen when you call from a mobile phone. So if you need an ambulance, call from a landline if possible. It can save valuable seconds.

SENDING HELP

At the ambulance dispatch centre, the call handler inputs the caller's information into a computer. The computer then grades the call – A, B or C. Grade A calls are the most urgent and need a paramedic within eight minutes. B calls need paramedic help, but not as urgently. C calls are not life-threatening.

A dispatcher uses the computer system to see what paramedic help is available closest to an emergency and then to send it out.

Dispatching

While a call handler is talking to a caller, he or she is passing the information to a **dispatcher**. The dispatcher's job is to send paramedic help to the emergency. The dispatcher also passes details of an emergency to the ambulance crew, so they know what to expect at the scene.

Helpful advice

Call handlers are specially trained to give first aid instructions over the phone. Their advice can help to keep a patient alive while paramedics are on their way.

FACE TO FACE

Tim – Call Handler

While I talk to callers, I key information into a computer. The computer shows me what questions I need to ask and helps me grade the calls. Sometimes the callers are frightened and panicky, and I have to calm them down.

By giving instructions over the phone, I've been able to help some people deliver babies safely and others to get seriously unwell patients breathing again. This work can be stressful, but I enjoy helping to save lives.

GETTING THERE FAST

The dispatcher radios the nearest paramedics to tell them to go to an emergency. Paramedics have a radio in their vehicle and also carry **alerters** with them at all times.

As soon as an emergency call comes in, a crew at the ambulance station quickly make their way to their vehicle and set off.

Every minute counts

In a medical emergency, a minute can make the difference between life and death. To help paramedics get to an emergency quickly, they have **satellite navigation (sat nav)** systems that tell the driver how to get there. Their vehicles have flashing lights and sirens that warn other motorists to pull over and let them through.

sat nav

This paramedic is pushing a button on the dashboard to sound the sirens on the ambulance.

999 Notes

If you are waiting for an ambulance to come to an emergency in your home, there are some things you can do to help the paramedics find you quickly:

- Open the doors
- If it is dark, turn on all the lights in and outside the house and pull back the curtains
- Ask someone to wait outside to signal to the ambulance
- If there are pets in the house, lock them into a room.

Rapid-response vehicles

Paramedics sometimes go to an emergency in cars, or on motorcycles or bicycles. These are called rapid-response vehicles (RRVs). They are smaller than ambulance vans, and can get through traffic quicker.

The bicycles are useful for moving through busy city centres or shopping malls. They are specially **adapted** to carry emergency equipment.

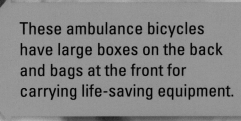

These ambulance bicycles have large boxes on the back and bags at the front for carrying life-saving equipment.

AMBULANCES AND RRVs

In most 999 emergencies, an ambulance is sent out with a crew of two people. One is a paramedic, while the other is usually an Emergency Care Assistant (ECA). An ECA is not as highly trained as a paramedic, but is able to give some medical aid and assist the paramedic.

First on the scene

Paramedics going out to an emergency in an RRV (a car, motorcycle or a bicycle) usually travel alone. They are sent ahead of an ambulance to give emergency treatment. Then the ambulance arrives to take the patient to hospital.

This type of RRV is sometimes used to take patients with minor injuries to hospital.

1034

AMBULANCE

RRVs may also be sent out as extra medical help at major emergencies. They may join ambulance crews at a road accident where several people are injured.

A motorcycle ambulance can get to a medical emergency in heavy traffic much faster than a car or van.

FACE TO FACE

Neville – Paramedic

My **shift** starts at the ambulance station in the morning or evening and lasts between 8 and 12 hours. I check the ambulance, the equipment and the supplies so we are ready to go as soon as we get a call.

Accidents, heart attacks and breathing difficulties are just some of the emergencies we go to. I have to decide quickly what treatment a patient needs. It might be dressing a wound, giving an injection or giving **life support** to keep a patient breathing.

HELP FROM THE AIR

Helicopters are used to send medical help and get patients to hospital in the fastest possible time. These air ambulances are particularly useful when there is an emergency far from a town or somewhere hard to reach by road.

When a patient has injuries to the head or spine, an air ambulance also avoids the jolting or bumping of travelling over uneven roads.

Helicopters on the road

Air ambulances are often called to serious road traffic accidents because queues of traffic make it difficult for a land ambulance to get there fast.

This patient is being put on a board with straps and blocks to prevent further damage to their spine.

An air ambulance usually has a crew of two or three people. This includes a pilot, at least one paramedic and sometimes a doctor. Paramedics who want to work on air ambulances have to learn about air safety and **navigation.** They are also trained to give more kinds of medical treatment than most other paramedics.

999 Notes

It costs more than one million pounds a year to run an air ambulance. Yet most air ambulances in the UK receive no money from the government. The service is paid for through **fund-raising** and money **donated** by local people and businesses.

AT THE AMBULANCE STATION

An ambulance station is the building where ambulances and rapid-response vehicles are based. A station in a small town may have just two emergency vehicles while bigger stations may have many more.

A fleet of ambulances and RRVs stand ready for action at a large ambulance station.

Ambulance stations have a garage where the vehicles are kept, and stores for equipment and medical supplies. There are lockers, changing rooms, showers and a kitchen area for staff.

The crew room is where staff hold meetings or relax between emergency call-outs.

Important checks

Emergency vehicles must be kept in good working order. At an ambulance station, the crew check the fuel, oil, water and tyres.

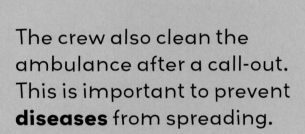

Mechanics are called in to fix any problems with the vehicles and to check them over.

The crew also clean the ambulance after a call-out. This is important to prevent **diseases** from spreading.

A crew member uses **disinfectant** to kill any germs in the ambulance.

999 Notes

Some ambulances are stationed at large hospitals. You may also have seen them parked at the side of the road, away from an ambulance station or hospital. These places are called standby points. Ambulances wait at these spots so that if there is an emergency in the nearby area, they can get to it within a few minutes.

INSIDE AN AMBULANCE

Ambulances are designed to carry a patient safely to hospital and to allow a paramedic to give treatment during the journey. An ambulance has equipment that helps the crew move patients into the vehicle with very little lifting.

Ambulances have a stretcher on wheels (below) and a ramp or small lift (right) at the back of the ambulance.

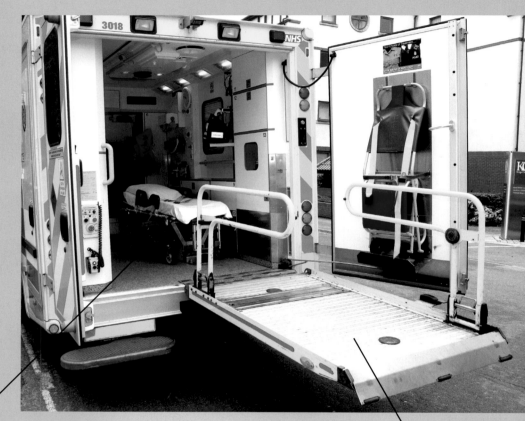

stretcher

lift

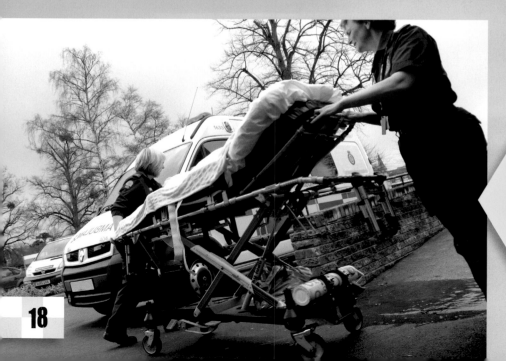

Stretchers on wheels allow ambulance crews to move patients safely and easily, without the risk of causing further injury.

Grab bags

All the supplies and equipment that a paramedic might need is stored in the ambulance. Some of it is stored in 'grab bags'. There are different grab bags for different types of emergencies, such as burns or someone giving birth.

Storing kit in a grab bag, like this, means that a paramedic doesn't waste time gathering together the right type of equipment.

heart monitor

defibrillator

Life-saving machines

An ambulance has to carry lots of life-saving equipment. On board is a heart monitor, used to show a paramedic how regularly or fast a person's heart is beating. Attached to this machine is a **defibrillator** (left) that uses an electric shock to restart a heart that has stopped beating.

999 Notes

An ambulance's **two-way radio** is one of its most important pieces of equipment. The dispatch centre gives the crew details of an emergency call over the radio. The crew use it to warn a hospital they are bringing in a seriously ill patient.

AN EMERGENCY CALL-OUT

The crew get an emergency call to go to a park where a boy is having a very bad asthma attack. Asthma causes difficulty breathing and an attack can be very serious if not treated quickly. The ambulance sets off with lights flashing and sirens wailing. When they arrive, the paramedic quickly picks up the correct grab bag and rushes to the patient.

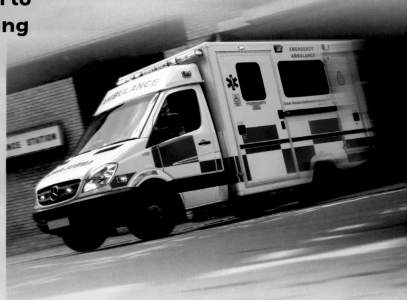

Quick treatment

First, the paramedic gives the patient **oxygen** through a mask to make sure he gets all the oxygen his body needs (left). Then the patient is put into the ambulance and given a mixture of drugs and more oxygen through a mask. This opens up his **airways** and helps him breathe.

bag valve mask

oxygen canister

The paramedic squeezes a device called a bag valve mask to force oxygen into the patient's lungs.

To the hospital

The ECA radios the dispatch centre (below) to explain what is happening and that they are on their way to hospital.

At the hospital, the paramedic hands the patient over to the A&E staff and gives them details of the emergency. Then it's back to the station to get ready for the next call-out.

The sat nav system helps the driver find the fastest way to the hospital.

999 Notes

Asthma is a condition where the airways get narrow and blocked, making it hard to breathe. There are medical drugs that treat asthma by opening the airways. People who know they have asthma often have devices called **inhalers** or 'puffers' that send the drugs straight to the lungs. However, sometimes a bad asthma attack needs emergency medical treatment.

inhaler

21

EMERGENCY VOLUNTEERS

Some doctors and nurses give up their spare time to help ambulance crews at major emergencies. These **volunteers** have special training in on-the-spot emergency care. Their extra skills can be very valuable.

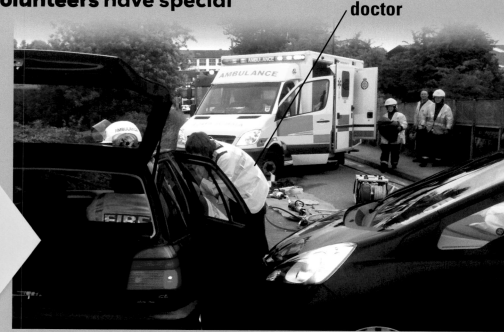

doctor

A doctor called to a crash scene might carry out life-saving surgery – something that most paramedics cannot do.

Local help

Another type of emergency aid comes from **Community Responders (CRs)** (left). These are members of the public trained to give emergency medical aid.

CRs are sent to incidents near where they live or work to provide help while an ambulance is on its way.

CRs are particularly useful in **rural** areas where there is no ambulance nearby. These people are also volunteers who work in their spare time and are not paid for what they do.

FACE TO FACE

Jo – Community Responder

Ambulance Community Responder

I work in a factory during the day and as a Community Responder in my spare time. I am one of eight responders in the area where I live. We work on a **rota**, taking turns to be on call.

Sometimes I get no calls during a shift; other times I may get two or three. I've helped at many different types of emergency – from heart attacks to falls. I like doing this work because I am helping the people where I live.

HART

Sometimes injured people are trapped in dangerous surroundings. This can happen when a building collapses or catches fire, or when a bomb has exploded. In the past, paramedics had to wait for casualties to be brought out of a danger area before treating them. Today, ambulance services often have Hazardous Area Response Teams (HART).

Danger zones

HART teams are made up of paramedics specially chosen and trained to help casualties inside dangerous areas. The paramedics learn safe ways of working in hazardous environments and how to use special equipment to reach a patient safely.

HART paramedics work closely with the fire and rescue services inside danger areas. They are on hand to treat any casualties.

New skills

To reach someone trapped in a building that is on fire, the paramedics need to learn how to use **breathing apparatus**. They also need to have practised skills, such as being able to give injections, while wearing heavy protective clothing. Giving life-saving treatment on the spot means casualties have a better chance of surviving.

999 Notes

From time to time, HART units from all over the country join together to take part in training exercises. A major incident scene is set up with real people taking the parts of casualties. This gives the teams a chance to try out their skills in a realistic situation.

In this training exercise, HART paramedics practise treating casualties when dangerous chemicals or poisons have been released into the air.

SUPER PARAMEDICS

Some paramedics do extra training to become Emergency Care Practitioners – sometimes called 'super paramedics'. This extra training means ECPs can carry out tests on patients and give them medical drugs that paramedics cannot normally give. They can also stitch up wounds at the scene.

Help at home

ECPs are usually based in doctors' surgeries or at hospitals. They may be sent to help other paramedics at a serious emergency. Often they are sent to patients who need attention, but whose lives are not in immediate danger. An ECP can choose to treat someone at home or send them to hospital.

An Emergency Care Practitioner takes the temperature of a young boy in his home.

The help that ECPs give means that fewer ambulances get called to non-emergencies. It also means that fewer people make unnecessary trips to hospital.

FACE TO FACE

Mike – Emergency Care Practitioner

I get called to all kinds of incidents: sick children, people who are in a lot of pain or elderly people who have fallen. Often, I can treat them in their own home, give advice or organise help for them. For elderly or weak people, this is usually much better than going to hospital.

One minute I may be stitching up a small cut, the next I may be going to a road traffic accident. There's plenty of variety in my job.

NON-EMERGENCY WORK

Patient transport services (PTS) is another important part of ambulance work. This often involves taking patients to and from hospital appointments. The service is for patients who have disabilities or are too unwell to travel any other way. It is also used to take patients home after a hospital stay.

PTS ambulances are driven by ambulance care assistants. They are skilled in moving patients and are trained in first aid. Some PTS are for carrying passengers on stretchers. Other types carry wheelchair users or are for people who just need help getting in and out of hospital.

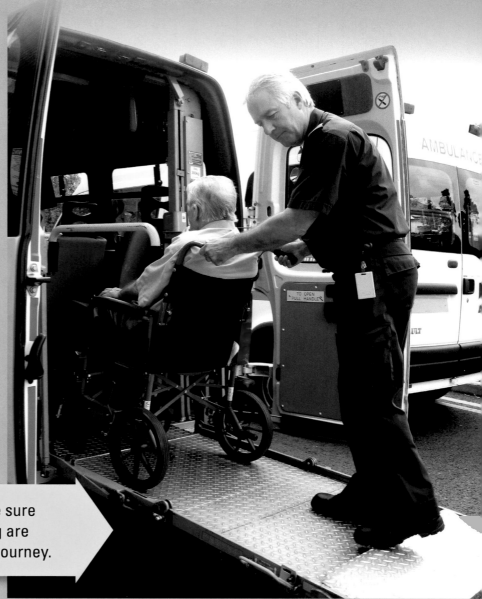

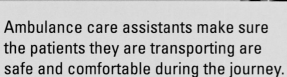

Ambulance care assistants make sure the patients they are transporting are safe and comfortable during the journey.

At the end of a marathon, event paramedics are on hand to treat a runner who is feeling unwell.

Event paramedics

Festivals, concerts, horse or car races, fêtes and many other kinds of events could not happen without paramedics. Organisers have to make sure that expert medical help is on hand for anyone who becomes ill or injured. They hire paramedics with ambulances or **portable** medical centres to provide this.

999 Notes

Paramedics visit schools to talk about their work with the ambulance service. They also explain what to do in a medical emergency. Sometimes they work with people from other emergency services to teach children how to deal with everyday dangers.

DO YOU HAVE WHAT IT TAKES?

To become a paramedic you can apply for a place as a student paramedic with an ambulance service. People who get a place will spend three years training and studying while they work with ambulance crews. Another way to become a paramedic is to go to university and study paramedic science for two years.

Paramedics must have a normal driving licence, but they need a licence to drive larger vehicles and carry passengers as well. Paramedics also need to be fit and strong as they may need to lift patients.

Could you be a paramedic?
Look at the following questions and answer 'yes' or 'no'.

- Are you interested in how the human body works and willing to study hard?
- Are you happy dealing with all types of people?
- Would you be willing to work days, nights and weekends?
- Would you be willing to go out in all weathers?
- Are you prepared to deal with people who may be difficult, rude or even violent?
- Do you enjoy working as part of a team?
- Can you stay calm in an emergency?
- Can you cope with seeing people who are very unwell or badly injured?
- Are you good at making quick decisions?

If you answered 'yes' to all these questions, then maybe one day you could be a paramedic!

GLOSSARY

Accident and Emergency (A&E) the part of a hospital where people go when they need medical treatment quickly

adapted changed to make something suitable for a particular use

airways the passages through which air travels from the mouth and nose to the lungs

alerter a small device that bleeps or vibrates to let you know that someone wishes to contact you

breathing apparatus a container filled with air, strapped to a person's back and attached by a tube to a face mask. It helps emergency workers breathe safely in smoky areas

Community Responder (CR) a local volunteer who is trained to give basic medical help in an emergency

conscious awake and aware of your surroundings

defibrillator a machine used to give an electric shock to the heart, to help it beat normally

disease sickness or illness

disinfectant a chemical liquid used to destroy the germs on something

dispatcher someone whose job is to contact paramedics or other help and send them to an emergency

donated given as a gift

first aid the emergency care given to a sick or injured person before skilled medical help is available

fund-raising activities or events organised to raise money for a good cause

inhaler a container for medicine that you take by breathing it in

landline a phone that is not mobile

life support techniques used to keep the vital parts of a patient's body working

navigation using maps or instruments to guide an aircraft or ship

oxygen one of the gases that is in the air we breathe and that we need for our bodies to work properly

paramedic person who is trained to do medical work

portable easy to move from place to place

pulse a steady beat that shows that blood is pumping through your body

rota a list of names showing how people take their turns to do duties

rural to do with the countryside

satellite navigation (sat nav) equipment used in vehicles to tell you how to get to a particular place

shift the period of hours that a group of people work

two-way radio a radio that can both receive and transmit messages

unconscious not awake and not responding to your surroundings

volunteer a person who does a job without pay

INDEX AND FURTHER INFORMATION

Websites

The West Midlands Ambulance Service has some advice about making 999 calls: **http://www.wmas.nhs.uk/our_services.aspx**

Find out about what to do in a medical emergency and how to give first aid on this Australian website (note, the emergency number given is 000 – in the UK this is 999 or 112): **http://www.cyh.com/HealthTopics/HealthTopicDetailsKids. aspx?p=335&id=1567**

Test your knowledge of first aid with a quiz on this cbbc website: **http://news.bbc. co.uk/cbbcnews/hi/newsid_4570000/newsid_4573400/4573493.stm**

Books

Ambulance Crew (People Who Help Us), Honor Head, Wayland, 2010
Ambulance Crews (People Who Help Us), Clare Oliver, Franklin Watts, 2002
In The Ambulance Service (Helping Hands), Ruth Thomson, Wayland, 2008